CELEBRATING THE CITY OF LONDON

Celebrating the City of London

Walter the Educator

Silent King Books

SILENT KING BOOKS

SKB

Copyright © 2024 by Walter the Educator

All rights reserved. No part of this book may be reproduced in any manner whatsoever without written permission except in the case of brief quotations embodied in critical articles and reviews.

First Printing, 2024

Disclaimer
This book is a literary work; the story is not about specific persons, locations, situations, and/or circumstances unless mentioned in a historical context. Any resemblance to real persons, locations, situations, and/or circumstances is coincidental. This book is for entertainment and informational purposes only. The author and publisher offer this information without warranties expressed or implied. No matter the grounds, neither the author nor the publisher will be accountable for any losses, injuries, or other damages caused by the reader's use of this book. The use of this book acknowledges an understanding and acceptance of this disclaimer.

Celebrating the City of London is a souvenir book that belongs to the Celebrating Cities Book Series by Walter the Educator. Collect them all and more books at WaltertheEducator.com

LONDON

In the heart of time where rivers wind and bend,

Celebrating the City of
London

A city stands, eternal, blending end to end,

Celebrating the City of London

London, ancient breath of whispers, modern dreams,

Celebrating the City of London

Through history's veil, her gilded skyline gleams.

Celebrating the City of London

Where cobblestones remember each shadow cast,

Celebrating the City of
London

And every tower tells the tales of ages past,

Celebrating the City of London

The Thames, a silver ribbon, serpentine,

Celebrating the City of London

Reflects the pulse of life in glittering line.

Celebrating the City of
London

Her bridges span the epochs, iron, and stone,

Celebrating the City of
London

Connecting hearts and stories all her own,

Celebrating the City of London

From Tower's watch to Westminster's chime,

Celebrating the City of London

The cadence of her streets, a metered rhyme.

Celebrating the City of
London

In fog's embrace, the spires ascend to sky,

Celebrating the City of
London

Old ghosts of kings and poets wandering by,

Celebrating the City of London

Through narrow lanes where secrets softly fall,

Celebrating the City of London

Brick and mortar whispering history's call.

Celebrating the City of
London

Beneath the dome of St. Paul's majestic grace,

Celebrating the City of London

The echoes of resilience find their place,

Celebrating the City of London

In markets bustling, voices interlace,

Celebrating the City of London

A tapestry of cultures, race by race.

Celebrating the City of
London

The East End's grit, the West End's shining light,

Celebrating the City of
London

In every corner, stories, dark and bright,

Celebrating the City of
London

From Camden's quirky soul to Mayfair's flair,

Celebrating the City of
London

A symphony of life flows everywhere.

Celebrating the City of London

In Hyde Park's greens and Kew's enchanting blooms,

Celebrating the City of London

In the quiet of the British Library's rooms,

Celebrating the City of London

Imagination soars on feathered wings,

Celebrating the City of
London

In London, where the muse forever sings.

Celebrating the City of London

Her museums guard the relics of the earth,

Celebrating the City of
London

Treasures of the past, of countless worth,

Celebrating the City of London

In every gallery, a portal through,

Celebrating the City of London

A glimpse of worlds that history withdrew.

Celebrating the City of London

From Big Ben's toll to Shard's ascending spire,

Celebrating the City of
London

Innovation dances with desire,

Celebrating the City of
London

Her theaters, where the bard's own words ignite,

Celebrating the City of
London

The dreams and passions of the endless night.

Celebrating the City of London

Oh, London, in your veins the world does flow,

Celebrating the City of
London

In every street, the seeds of dreams do grow,

Celebrating the City of
London

A haven where the old and new embrace,

Celebrating the City of
London

A timeless epic, written in your grace.

Celebrating the City of London

ABOUT THE CREATOR

Walter the Educator is one of the pseudonyms for Walter Anderson. Formally educated in Chemistry, Business, and Education, he is an educator, an author, a diverse entrepreneur, and he is the son of a disabled war veteran. "Walter the Educator" shares his time between educating and creating. He holds interests and owns several creative projects that entertain, enlighten, enhance, and educate, hoping to inspire and motivate you.

> Follow, find new works, and stay up to date
> with Walter the Educator™
> at WaltertheEducator.com

Milton Keynes UK
Ingram Content Group UK Ltd.
UKHW020725110724
445228UK00013B/467